Ma
Carole Conway
Carole Wynne

All the praise, all the thanks, all the glory to Your name, all for You, Jesus.

THANK YOU, GOD, FOR CHOOSING ME

To Marilyn
Praying this book speaks to you about how much God loves you + has planned for you!
♥ Ashton Duffrenne

contents

Introduction	4
Sarah	6
Leah	11
Rachel	16
Rahab	20
Eve	25
Hannah	30
Promise: Part One	35
Promise: Part Two	40
Ruth	45
Esther	50
Phoebe	55
Mary Magdalene: Intro	62
Mary Magdalene: Part One	67
Mary Magdalene: Part Two	72
Judges 4: Part One	77
Judges 4: Part Two	82
Deborah & Jael	87
Bleeding Woman	92
Mary of Bethany	97
Abigail	102
Shattered Pride	108
The Father	113
Mary, Mother of Jesus	118
Elizabeth	123
The Samaritan Woman	127
Martha	132
Rebekah	137
Stay with the Cloud	142
Enter In	147
Huldah	152

INTRODUCTION

I began writing these devotionals because there had been a stirring in my Spirit to study the Women of God in the Bible. It was sparked when I was listening to Church of the Highland's Children's Pastor, Beth Cunningham, and she said that many women are asking the question, "Am I called? and if I am, to what?" She did not have the time to elaborate much, but she essentially answered that question with a list of women from the Bible and what they were used by God to do.

I left that night feeling empowered as a female leader, and throughout the following week, I could not get the question she presented off of my heart: "Are women called, and if so, to what?"

My heart began to feel heavy for the women that may be answering that question based upon religious barriers, their pasts, the words of man, self-doubt, or anything else that was not the Word of God.

God began prompting me to really study all the women in the Bible, not just the main heroines we always think of. He has revealed that we can learn so much from these women if we take the time to look, so I decided to write the things God has revealed to me and share them with you. I have come to find that God used women all throughout the Bible. So, **in answering the question, "Are women called?," I would have to respond with "They always were."**

I pray that God stirs something up in you as you read about the women in His Word. I pray he reveals the things He wants to use you for because woman of God, you are called to so much more than you know.

DAY ONE

SARAH

FIGHTING YOUR DOUBT

GENESIS 17-21

Now the Lord was gracious to Sarah as He had said, and the Lord did for Sarah what He had promised.

Genesis 21:1

NIV

There is so much to unpack with Sarah. She is the wife of Abraham, the Father of Israel. If you're familiar with the story, you may remember or were taught that God changed the name of Abram to Abraham when he made the covenant, but something I didn't realize is that God also changed his wife's name from Sarai to Sarah. I found this interesting and confusing at first because Sarah and Sarai both mean "princess." I wondered why God would bother changing her name to something that meant the same thing, and then it hit me: God was about to make her a princess with a kingdom.

By giving her a name that still meant "princess," God was affirming in her that her name was no accident. She may not have seen the fruit yet, because she had not yet had children, but God was going to use her to be the mother of His Kingdom and begin the line from which the King of Kings would be born!

Sarah was 90 years old when she received the promise of a son. We don't really get to hear much about the other 89 years of her life, but I wonder if she had spent them praying for children. I wonder if she had begun living in the identity that the world had given her: barren.

Sometimes, that is an easy identity to take on. We pray and pray for something, and when it doesn't come, we sink into the disappointment and suddenly no fruit can grow in our lives.

I imagine Sarah may have found herself in this place before, so when she heard that she was supposed to give birth at the age of 90, I can understand why her first response was doubt. "She laughed silently to herself and said, "How could a worn-out woman like me enjoy such pleasure, especially when my master—my husband—is also so old?'" Genesis 18:12 NIV.

Sarah had the wrong view of herself. She saw herself as "worn-out," and her wrong view of herself became a lens through which she began to view God. Instead of thinking about who God was, she began to get caught up in who she wasn't. (Relate? Me too.)

The absolute beautiful thing about our God, though, is that Sarah's doubt did not stop God's calling on her life. God knew how long she had waited. He knew she was only human. So, His response to her doubt was: "Is anything too hard for the Lord? I will return about this time next year, and Sarah will have a son" Genesis 18:14 NIV.

In Mark 9, there is a father asking for his son to be freed of the demon possessing him. When Jesus tells him anything is possible for those who believe, he responds with "I do believe, but help me overcome my unbelief" (Mark 9:24 NLT). The son is freed despite his father's doubt.

God has not called you to never doubt; He has called you to never stop asking Him to help you overcome your doubt. When we sink into our doubt, we're left barren. When we fight it, we open the door for a miracle.

Reflection:

- Is there a false identity that you've found yourself living in?

- Has a wrong view of yourself polluted your view of God?

- What doubts are you facing in your life right now? Write a prayer asking God to help you overcome them and trust Him fully.

DAY TWO

LEAH

GREATER THAN YOUR PLANS

GENESIS 29 & 30

When the Lord saw that Leah was not loved, He enabled her to conceive.

Genesis 29:31

NIV

Leah, her story is one that I've heard so many times, but I've always heard it from the "Jacob Perspective." Jacob was the father of Israel, through which God's covenant with Abraham would be fulfilled. Jacob loved Rachel, Leah's sister. Jacob was deceived by Rachel's father and given Leah as a wife even though he was supposed to get Rachel after he worked his 7 years for their father. Jacob was finally given Rachel too, but he had to work another 7 years. How sad for Jacob, but at least he finally got the beautiful Rachel.

I had never read their story zoomed in on the women until I started this Women of the Bible study, and what I saw was beautiful.

So, the first thing the Bible says about the two women is that Rachel had a beautiful figure and a lovely face, and Leah had no sparkle in her eyes, (ouch). I feel like all of us at one time or another have felt like we were a Leah in a sea of Rachels. We look around at all the women who look the way the world says they're "supposed to look" and feel no sparkle in our eyes. If I had to guess, I would say that Leah probably struggled with something that many of us do: Comparison.

Leah probably saw her sister Rachel and wondered why God didn't make her look more like that. She was also the oldest, which meant she was supposed to get married first, but her sister was the one men desired. I wonder how many men came through wanting Rachel instead of Leah before Jacob got there. She finally gets married, and it has to be through deception? How is this fair?

Honestly, reading her story was pretty frustrating. The Bible even says that Jacob loved Rachel much more than Leah, so why is this beautiful?

Genesis 29:31 NIV- When the Lord saw that Leah was not loved, He enabled her to conceive, but Rachel remained childless.

The Lord saw Leah. He not only saw her, but he cared. The Lord knew that back in those days, a wife was only valued by society if she could bear sons, so he gave her four in a row and two more later. They were all confirmations that the Lord saw her, and even though he eventually did let Rachel have children, he let Leah have them first.

Is this the exact ending Leah wanted? Probably not. I'm sure she would have wanted a husband who loved her the most, but instead, she birthed the majority of the tribes of Israel, including Judah, which Jesus would be born from! God's plans were bigger than hers. God saw her. God sees you. His plans are bigger than ours. Leah planned to get married and have children; God planned for Leah to get married and birth His nation, the lineage His son would come from.

Leah did not know during her lifetime that the Savior of the world would come from her bloodline. Often times, we cannot know the beauty within the story that the Lord is writing through us, but here is something you can know: you are called to something greater than your plans.

Reflection:

- Have you found yourself becoming consumed by comparison?

- Do you fully believe and fully know that the Lord sees you and cares for you?

- Do you struggle releasing your plans? Write a prayer asking God to help you lay your plans on the altar, trusting that His plans are greater than yours.

DAY THREE

RACHEL

FEED HIS SHEEP

GENESIS 29 & 30

While he was still talking with them, Rachel came with her father's sheep, for she was a shepherd.

Genesis 29:9

NIV

Yesterday you read about Leah; today, I want to talk about her sister, Rachel.
The question that sparked this study was "Are women called? & if so, to what?"

While reading Rachel's story, I noticed something I never had before: Rachel was a shepherd. This was the first time I remembered seeing that a woman was a shepherd, and it made me wonder "Was it unusual for women to be shepherds?"
After doing some research [a], I've found that the answer was absolutely not. The job of shepherdess was actually *reserved* for young girls. They would start when they were about 9 or 10 years old and work the flocks until they were married off at 15 or 16.

I began thinking about how Jesus uses a shepherd to describe the way He loves and guides His people throughout the Bible. He calls Himself the Good Shepherd in John 10 because He would lay His life down for His people, the same way a shepherd will throw themselves between their sheep and a lion.

When Jesus asks Peter, "Do you love me?" in John 21 NLT, Peter replies, "You know I love you." And what does Jesus respond with? "Then feed my sheep."

So, Woman of God, what are you called to do? Feed His sheep. You are not disqualified or excused from this assignment because you are a woman. In fact, you are empowered to do it because there are assignments, messages, and missions *reserved* for you.

Ephesians 2:10 NLT "For we are God's masterpiece. He has created us anew in Christ Jesus, so we can do the good things he planned for us long ago."

a: *Occupations of Bible Women - Life as a Shepherdess.* WomenfromtheBook Blog. (2012, October 29). Retrieved August 3, 2021, from https://womenfromthebook.com/category/occupations-of-bible-women/

Reflection:

- What does it mean to "Feed God's Sheep"?

- How can you practically "Feed His Sheep" in your every day life?

- Have you ever felt disqualified to share the Gospel, share your testimony, prayer over someone, or even share a Word from God that you received? Write a prayer asking God to help you feel empowered to be His witness. Ask Him to give you a fresh boldness when it comes to leading and caring for His people.

DAY FOUR

RAHAB

MORE THAN YOUR MISTAKES

JOSHUA 2

For the Lord your God is the supreme God of the heavens above and the earth below.

Joshua 2:11b

NLT

I love Rahab's story. To sum her up, she was a prostitute that had heard what the God of Israel had been doing, so when His people came knocking, she opened the door.

You ever wonder why the Bible includes certain details? While studying Rahab, I wondered why God thought it was important to say the "spies came to the house of a prostitute named Rahab" instead of just saying "Rahab's house."
Something that I learned in my Religion classes at the University of North Alabama (UNA) is that if it is included in the Bible, it's important. When a detail was included, it was because that detail was supposed to do something: remind you of another story, stir something up in you, allude to something in the future, etc.

So, why include that she was a prostitute? Well, I think it was for me. I think it was for you. I think it was so that when our callings came knocking, you and I couldn't use our past or present sins or mistakes as an excuse to disqualify ourselves from being involved in what God was about to do.

She knew who her shame said she was, but she also knew something else: (Rehab speaking) "For the Lord your God is the supreme God of the heavens above and the earth below" Joshua 2:11 NLT. She knew who God was, and if the supreme God of the heavens and earth decided she would be the one He would send His people to for protection then she would answer the door. She answered the door knowing it could cost her everything, knowing people would say she was unworthy, knowing what she had done yesterday, but also knowing stepping out in faith could save her life.

God always does exceedingly, abundantly above all that we ask or think. He didn't stop with her salvation, although that would've been enough. No, while the world looked on her as dirty, unworthy, shameful, God saw her as chosen. He saw through all her mess and mistakes and saw who she could be: part of His son's lineage. She became the great great grandmother of King David.

This is what the Heavenly Father does for his daughters: He takes their rags of shame and replaces them with robes of royalty.

Your calling will not be taken away because of your mistakes.

Reflection:

- Have you ever felt like your past disqualified you from God's presence?

- Do you believe that there is no sin or mistake that you could make that would ever cause God to love you any less, think less of you, or lose His pride in you? (Romans 8:38-39 NIV)

- Are there any mistakes in your past or your present that cause you to feel shameful or disqualified? Write a prayer asking God to forgive you and help you forgive yourself. Ask Him to remove the heavy weight of shame and replace it with a blanket of Mercy.

DAY FIVE

EVE

STILL CHOSEN

GENESIS 2 & 3

Adam named his wife Eve, because she would become the mother of all the living.

Genesis 3:20

NIV

I feel like Eve really gets an unfair judgement. Throughout history, I think people have judged her because of what she did instead of why she did it.
Growing up, I had always heard people say that Eve brought sin into the world. That it was the "woman's fault" (as if her husband wasn't standing right beside her when it happened, but that's beside the point). We blame poor Eve for suffering and a fallen world when really she was just a victim of Satan's lies like we all have been before. Her heart was even in a good place, which to me, turns Eve's story into a warning for women, not a condemnation for them.

One of the most profound things I ever heard someone teach about Eve was from Pastor Chris Hodges in the Freedom curriculum [b] that we have at Church of the Highlands. See, Eve didn't want to eat from the forbidden tree to spite God, rebel, get revenge, or anything like that. She wanted to eat from it because Satan said, "You will be like God" (Genesis 3:5 NIV). She just wanted to be more like her Father.
It was innocent. It was pure. It was a well devised trap.

Here's where the warning comes in, Women of God: you *have* to *know* what God said and never compromise on it.

Satan is not that original. He has been using the same lie since the garden: "Did God *really* say?" (Genesis 3:1 NIV). If you don't know who God says you are, if you don't know what God says is good, if you don't know how God says to live, you will be vulnerable to the seed of doubt.
Where do we find out what God said? His Word.

b: Hodges, C. (n.d.). *Freedom Curriculum.*

I began this study on the Women in the Bible because I became desperate to know everything God's Word said about women: how He used them, what He saw in them, where He sent them, what He said about them.

Here's what I've found in this story: Eve was not targeted by Satan because she was weaker, less than, or loved any less by her Father. Eve was targeted because she was hungry for God. Satan only attacks what he feels threatened by, & the first person he attacked was a woman walking closely with her Heavenly Father, longing to be more like Him.

I wonder what scared him the most about Eve. I wonder what scares him the most about you.
If Satan doesn't disqualify you as a threat because you're a woman, why would you disqualify yourself?

Here's the most important part of Eve's story. Although Eve fell for the lie and sinned, God did not take away who He called her to be. It was after her sin that she was named Eve, which means "to give life" because God chose her to be the mother of all who live (Genesis 3:20 NLT). It would've been very easy for God to create a different woman for the world to be born from, one who didn't mess up, but that was not our Father's heart.

Maybe you've messed up and feel like your calling will be given to someone else. Daughter of the King, that is not our Father's heart. You are still chosen.

Reflection:

- How often do you spend intentional time with God?

- What lie has Satan been trying to convince you of? What seeds of doubt has Satan been planting in your mind?

- Have you ever felt like your mistakes messed up God's plan for you? Write a prayer thanking God that there is nothing you could ever do to mess up His plans. Ask Him to reveal opportunities for you to minister to other women who have perhaps made the same mistakes you made.

DAY SIX

HANNAH

KEEP ASKING

1 SAMUEL 1

the Lord remembered her. So in the course of time Hannah became pregnant and gave birth to a son. She named him Samuel, saying, "Because I asked the Lord for him."

1 Samuel 1:19b-20

NIV

Hannah was someone who knew what it meant to pursue God in prayer. She had been desperately craving a son, and she was honestly very alone in her pursuit of this blessing.

Hannah's husband did not even understand why she wanted children. He thought he should be enough for her. Hannah's husband had another wife named Elkanah, and she was blessed with many children. Elkanah would taunt Hannah for not having any children, and it would reduce Hannah to tears, to the point where she couldn't eat.

Maybe you've felt like Hannah. You've been desperately praying for something (a healing, a calling, clarity, breakthrough, reconciliation, freedom, etc), and it seems like, instead of hearing God answer that prayer, you only hear the voices taunting you for praying it in the first place. You've been pleading with God, and it seems like nothing has changed. Well, Woman of God, this is your sign that Heaven hears you, and breakthrough is closer than you know.

Hannah was brought to a moment where her heart shifted; she realized that the gifts God gives us never stop being His.
She promised to give the one thing she wanted most right back to the Lord if he would bless her with it, and after she made this promise, the Bible says, "she was no longer sad" (1 Samuel 1:18 NLT).
There is a peace that comes when we realize that prayer is about keeping our hands open to the Lord, even after He puts what we prayed for into them.

Hannah kept her promise, and the Lord kept His.
She was blessed with a son named Samuel, and she only kept him until he was old enough to be weaned, then she brought him to the Tabernacle as she promised.

Hannah walked away that day knowing that she may have just parted with the only child she would ever have, but here's the beautiful heart of our Father: He had more for her than that. God blessed Hannah with 3 more sons and 2 daughters.

I'm not sure what you're praying for right now. I'm not sure what request has brought you to tears lately. Here's what I am sure of: Your Heavenly Father has *more for you*, so don't stop asking Him.

Reflection:

- What have you been desperately praying for?

- Have you started to lose faith that God will answer your prayer? If so, why?

- Do you believe that God is good and everything He does is good? (Psalm 119:68 NIV) Write a prayer asking God to help you trust Him fully with what you're praying for. Ask Him to give you the faith to believe that He does hear your prayer, He is going to answer it, and the way He answers it will be good.

DAY SEVEN

PROMISE

PART ONE:
PREPARE TO PROSPER

Don't overlook the obvious here, friends. With God, one day is as good as a thousand years, a thousand years as a day. **God isn't *late* with His *promise* as some measure lateness.**
He is restraining Himself on account of you, holding back the End because He doesn't want anyone lost. He's giving everyone space & time to change.

2 Peter 3:8-9 MSG

As I read these verses, something jumped out at me. "God isn't late with his promise as some measure lateness. He is restraining himself on account of you."

The actual context of this verse is the second coming of Christ. Paul is saying that Christ is coming, and though you expected Him to have come already, He is holding back so that more people have time to repent and go to Heaven.
When I read it, though, God spoke something different to me.

I love that God's Word is alive, always speaking if we're willing to listen. As I read these verses, I thought about the promises I feel that I have received from God, many of which I thought would have already come to pass by now.

Maybe you feel the same way. Maybe you're waiting on your promise: your calling, your husband, a child, a friend group, etc. I love the beautiful explanation of why those things have not yet come to fruition: on account of you.

Now, don't hear me wrong. This does not mean that it hasn't happened yet because of something we're not doing, but because of someone we have not yet become.
God is not withholding your promise for your punishment, but for your benefit.

God is not late with His promise. He has not yet given it to you because if you received it now, it wouldn't be everything that it could be.

Take the story of David for instance. He received the promise from God that he would become the King of Israel when he was around 15 years old. David did not take the throne until he was 30. Why? Because God was going to take some time to shape and prepare David for the promise he would receive.
The prosperity David saw in his reign required some preparation.

The fact that you haven't received the promise does not mean it's no longer yours. It just means God loves you enough to prepare you so that your promise can prosper, so lean into it.

God is a man of His word; He keeps His promises.
Take heart, trust Him, the promise is coming.

Reflection:

- What promise from God are you waiting on?

- What are some practical ways you can remind yourself daily of God's promise?

- Are you allowing God to grow you in your waiting season? Write a prayer asking God to grow you into the person He designed you to be during your waiting season. Ask Him to show you your next steps and help you remain confident that He is a man of His word.

DAY EIGHT

PROMISE

PART TWO:
REMEMBER WHAT'S ON YOU

So as David stood there among his brothers, Samuel took the flask of olive oil he had brought & anointed David with the oil.

& the Spirit of the LORD came powerfully upon David *from that day on.*

1 SAMUEL 16:13
NIV

When I begin to think about the promises of God, I often find myself thinking about King David. His life gives us such a great picture of what we should do in between the promise and the fruition of it.

You can look at the list of things that happened in between his promise and the fruition of it and wonder how he did it. How did he not lose hope? How did he not give up? How did he stay humble, kind, and compassionate?

Well, I think the answer lies in 1 Samuel 16:13 "So as David stood there among his brothers, Samuel took the flask of olive oil he had brought and anointed David with the oil. And the Spirit of the Lord came powerfully upon David from that day on."

Sometimes it can be easy to forget that the Spirit of the Lord is on you in the between. You don't have to wait until the promise is fulfilled for God to use you; His spirit is on you now.
That's how David went to war in his waiting: he knew what was on him.

When we remember that the Spirit of the Lord is on us now, it becomes abundantly clear that the promise we have received is not a destination. It is not something we have to wait on. It is not your starting line or your finish line. It is simply one of the many gifts God has prepared for you.

Don't spend your life waiting to receive one gift when God has so many others for you in the meantime.

You feel called to do something for God? Allow Him to do something with you in the meantime.
You feel called to be a mother? Be a spiritual mother to the children around you in the meantime.
You feel called to be a wife? Allow God to shape you and use your singleness in the meantime.

If you allow your promise from God to have too much weight, it will become your God.
I've made that mistake before. God had to reveal to me that the only thing I wasn't willing to lay on the alter a few years ago was my calling. When we get to this place, we've missed the point.

Don't worry about your promise; God wants to fulfill it. You need only to remember what's on you.

Reflection:

- What has your heart: the promise or the Promise Giver?

- What are some practical ways you can step into your calling in your day to day life?

- Do you know that the Spirit of the Lord is already on you and wanting to use you? Write a prayer asking God to help you recognize and access His Spirit's power every day. Ask Him to show you ways to step into your calling today through the power of His Spirit.

DAY NINE

RUTH

BETTER THAN BEFORE

BOOK OF RUTH

Boaz took Ruth and she became his wife. When he made love to her, the Lord enabled her to conceive, and she gave birth to a son. And they named him Obed. He was the father of Jesse, the father of David.

Ruth 4:13 & 17b

NIV

Have you ever felt like something was taken away from you? Maybe it was a person, or maybe an opportunity, or a dream, your joy, your peace, or your hope.
If you've felt this way, Ruth can relate. Ruth lost her husband, and in her time, it meant she'd lost all income, security, and safety as well.

Her mother-in-law, Naomi, was a Jew and heard that the Lord had blessed Judah with good crops, so she decided to go there. She told Ruth to go back to her people so she might remarry, but Ruth wouldn't go.
"Ruth replied, "Don't ask me to leave you and turn back. Wherever you go, I will go; wherever you live, I will live. Your people will be my people, and *your God will be my God*. Wherever you die, I will die, and there I will be buried. May the Lord punish me severely if I allow anything but death to separate us!" When Naomi saw that Ruth was determined to go with her, she said nothing more" (1:16-18 NLT)

It would have been very easy for Ruth to cling to comfort in the midst of loss. She could have gone back to her hometown, to the familiar, and taken the easier path.
But Ruth was determined.
Ruth recognized that even if she didn't get to remarry, a life lived among God's people would always be better.

Here's what we can learn from Ruth: Do Not Let Loss Push You Into Isolation.

God has always been in the business of taking what the enemy meant for evil and turning it for good. Sometimes our heartbreak is to keep us from settling for less than what God has for us. Sometimes our greatest pain will become the testimony that allows someone else to experience freedom. But it's hard in the moment ... So how do we stay focused on the right things?

Hebrews 10:23-25 NLT "Let us hold tightly without wavering to the hope we affirm, for God can be trusted to keep His promise. Let us think of ways to motivate one another to acts of love and good works and let us not neglect our meeting together, as some do, but encourage one another"

Community with God's people is how we stay focused. They will remind you that God can be trusted to keep His promise.

So, Ruth goes with Naomi to live among God's people, and what does she find among God's people? Restoration of what was lost.

She meets Boaz, her kinsman redeemer, who becomes her husband. With Boaz, she is also gifted with children that would begin the lineage that Jesus would be born from!

God's plan is not only to restore to you what was lost, but restore it better than before.

Reflection:

- Do you feel like something was taken away from you?

- Has the loss that you've experienced caused you to isolate yourself? This could be physically, emotionally, or spiritually.

- Do you believe that God can and will restore what you lost, better than before? Write a prayer asking God to help you believe that He is the God of restoration and that He causes everything to work together for the good of those who love Him (Romans 8:28 NLT). Ask Him to surround you with Godly community that will point you back to Him.

DAY TEN

ESTHER

ACCEPTING THE CALL

BOOK OF ESTHER

"For if you remain silent at this time, relief and deliverance for the Jews will arise from another place, but you and your father's family will perish. And who knows but that you have come to your royal position for such a time as this?"

Esther 4:14

NIV

Esther: truly one of my favorite stories in the Bible. There is so much to unpack here, and honestly, every time I read it I find another new thing.

Something that I had never seen before until reading this time zoomed in on women is that Esther's story starts because the King and his royal advisors fear the *influence of a woman*. Queen Vashti was summoned to the King, and she refused to come. Because of her refusal, they thought that all of the women in the entire kingdom would begin refusing orders from their husbands. The king's fear of this woman's influence sets this story into motion.
Woman of God, do not underestimate your influence.
Esther used her influence to save an entire nation. What will you use yours for?

Another thing that caught my eye for the first time about Esther was that she was an orphan. Mordecai was Esther's cousin, but the Bible says that he "adopted her into his family and raised her as his own daughter" (Esther 2:7 NLT).

The relationship of Esther and Mordecai reminded me of another adoptive relationship, between us and the Father. When we are adopted into the family of God, we are no longer orphans, but heirs and joint heirs with Jesus. He promises us in John 14:18 NIV, "I will not leave you as orphans; I will come to you."

The beautiful thing about Mordecai and Esther is that Mordecai never leaves Esther while she goes to fulfill her calling. "Every day Mordecai would take a walk near the courtyard of the harem to find out about Esther and what was happening to her" (2:11 NLT). They sent messages to each other, Mordecai prayed and fasted for her, and he never let her face this giant alone. In fact, it was the very same person that looked at her and said I will not leave you as an orphan that looked at her and said, "you have come to your position for such a time as this." (4:14 NIV)

As you come into your calling, the one who looked at you and said I will not leave you an orphan is also saying to you, "You have come to your position for such a time as this."

He will not leave you. He is here to talk with you, intercede for you, and never let you face your giants alone.

Esther was wise enough to invite people into her calling. She asked people to pray and fast for her, not because she was too weak to do it alone, but because she was strong enough to invite them.
It's okay to feel called to big things. It's okay to feel called to scary things. It's okay to not know what your calling will look like. Esther knew it was big, she knew it was scary, and she didn't know exactly what it would look like.

But here is our confidence, as we enter the throne room to accept the call, we never walk in alone.

"The LORD will go before you, and the God of Israel will be your rear guard" Isaiah 52:12 NIV.

Reflection:

- How are you using your influence? (in your workplace, in your family, in your friend group)

- Have you invited God and other believers into your calling: to walk with you, pray with you, and believe with you? If not, why?

- Is there anything you are being called to that feels scary or intimidating? Write a prayer asking God to give you the faith and boldness that you need to step into your calling. Ask God to send you the right believers to invite into the process with you, and ask God to go before you and behind you into this season.

DAY ELEVEN

PHOEBE

WRESTLING FOR A BLESSING

GENESIS 32:22-32 &
ROMANS 16:1-2

Jacob replied, "I will not let you go unless you bless me."

Genesis 32:26b

NIV

When I wrote this, we were in the middle of 21 Days of Prayer at Church of the Highlands. I found it very ironically fitting that the morning I would write this, Pastor Jamil would speak on wrestling with God in prayer, and the day before during my prayer time, I had one of the most raw wrestling with God moments I've ever had. (Read Genesis 32:22-32 NIV)

This Women of God study has honestly been one big wrestle with God for me. Although the Holy Spirit has revealed many amazing truths to me about women during this study, there are still things that God has yet to reveal.

A scripture that I've been disheartened by is:
1 Timothy 2:11-15 NLT "11 Women should learn quietly and submissively. 12 I do not let women teach men or have authority over them. Let them listen quietly. 13 For God made Adam first, and afterward he made Eve. 14 And it was not Adam who was deceived by Satan. The woman was deceived, and sin was the result. 15 But women will be saved through childbearing, assuming they continue to live in faith, love, holiness, and modesty."

This was what brought me to wrestle; to tears; to screaming; to anger; to frustration; to heaviness.

In my religion courses, we studied these verses and scholars teach that verses 11-12 was more about the time period than a general rule. Women weren't allowed to be educated, so this made them easy prey for the false teachers Paul warns about. Therefore, they shouldn't be allowed to teach because they may have been falsely informed. They would also interrupt the lectures with uneducated questions, which, in that time, was incredibly insulting to the speaker and a sign of disrespect.

I also agree that God created men to be leaders and the head of the household. These things I believe and have no issue with (especially when Paul addressed a female deacon named, Phoebe, in a letter, but that's for later).
No, it's verses 14-15 that brought me to wrestle.

Adam was standing right next to Eve when she was deceived. If men are called to lead us, why didn't he stop her? Why didn't he remind her of the truth? Why did he let them walk over to the tree to begin with? Why wasn't he leading better? Why didn't he protect her? Why did he eat the fruit too?! Why does she take all the blame?!
Is that really all we're good for?! Bearing children? Is this the only thing women can do? And what about all the mothers who crave a child but are left empty handed?

If that's not your heart, God, why did you allow this to be written?! "All scripture is God breathed" (2 Timothy 3:16 NIV) so explain yourself!

I felt my hip break. Like Jacob, I felt wounded from wrestling.

...

Still.
Psalm 46:10 NIV - Be still and know that I am God.

I suddenly fell still. I felt peace. Then, I remembered what they say is the most important rule of reading scripture: always read the entire thing, never just a few verses or you might miss it.

I was studying the next chapter in 1 Timothy and found something that felt like God's personal gift to me. (Jacob didn't release from wrestling until he received a blessing.)
The chapter is discussing deacons and church leadership.

1 Timothy 3:11 NLT "In the same way, their wives(e) must be respected and must not slander others. They must exercise self-control and be faithful in everything they do." [c]
That (e) is a note that says the word here in the original Greek could have been translated as wives or as women. So, the scripture could have read: In the same way as the male deacons, the women deacons must be …

And Phoebe is our example.
Romans 16:1-2 NLT "I commend to you our sister Phoebe, who is a deacon in the church in Cenchrea. Welcome her in the Lord as one who is worthy of honor among God's people. Help her in whatever she needs, for she has been helpful to many, and especially to me."

Just in case, I looked up what a deacon meant during that time: to serve and help lead the church as an official, similar to an overseer. [d]

I know this story isn't a very pretty one, but it's honest. I tell it because I want you to grasp hold of this truth:
We cannot point to one section of scripture taken out of the whole to learn what God thinks about anything, including women. Some want to say scripture is self-contradictory, but it's really not. It may seem that way piece to piece, but not whole.

c: *The Holy Bible.* Tyndale House Foundation. (2015). *1 Timothy 3.* 1 Timothy 3 NLT - Bible Gateway. Retrieved August 17, 2021, from https://www.biblegateway.com/passage/?search=1%2Btimothy%2B3&version=NLT
d: Strauch, Alexander. *Paul's Vision for the Deacons - Lewis & Roth Publishers.* 2017, https://lewisandroth.com/wp-content/uploads/sample-chapters-pauls-vision-for-the-deacons.pdf.

I also want you to grab hold of the truth that it is okay to wrestle with God. He knows that we're human. He knows we have questions, and He wants us to come to Him for the answers.

The bottom line is that God didn't think the world would be good without women. He's been using us since the beginning, and He will use us until the end.

Don't be afraid to wrestle, Woman of God. You're called to more than you know, and God has a blessing waiting for you.

Reflection:

- Have you ever felt discounted or restricted because of your gender? Do you have questions about things in Scripture?

Take some time and wrestle with God about those things. Search for Him in Scripture. Ask Him your questions and seek out the answers in His Word. Be honest with Him about how you feel. Get vulnerable before the Lord. Know this going in: The Lord is for you, He is proud of you, He loves you, He chooses you, He calls you, He anoints you, He created you, and He wants you to ask Him the questions you have. Use the space below to write your prayers, your questions, and the answers He reveals to you in His timing.

DAY TWELVE

MARY MAGDALENE

INTRO

LUKE 8:1-3

After this, Jesus traveled about from one town and village to another, proclaiming the good news of the kingdom of God. The Twelve were with Him, and also some women who had been cured of evil spirits and diseases: Mary (called Magdalene) from whom seven demons had come out.

Luke 8:1-2

NIV

Through this study, Mary Magdalene has become my favorite female character in the Bible. I believe her story encompasses everything women are called to and capable of, and it starts in Luke 8:1-3 NIV, the first time she's mentioned.

There is so much to unpack in these 3 verses. The first thing that I'd want you to see is that Jesus chose to take women with Him to preach the Good News. He chose to. They didn't follow him there unwanted; they were invited, and so are you.

The Bible says that these women had been cured of evil spirits and diseases, which tells us two things: 1. They had seen the goodness of God personally, and 2. They were not disqualified by what they had to be cured from.

I think sometimes it's easy for us to still feel discounted because of the things we have been cured from. We know we have freedom, we know we have healing, and yet, we still hear Satan's whispers that those things still matter. This is why I love Mary Magdalene's story so much.

When Jesus met Mary Magdalene, she was possessed by seven demons.
Seven is an interesting number in Scripture. It means and represents "completion." So, when Luke points out that Mary Magdalene had seven demons, he was emphasizing that she seemed completely gone, completely unworthy, completely hopeless. Maybe you've viewed yourself that way before, or even viewed someone else that way before.

The amazing thing is that Jesus never views anyone that way. When He saw Mary Magdalene, He just saw her as *Completely His*, so he made her completely whole.

I love that Mary Magdalene's story starts this way. She is redeemed, made whole, and then she doesn't let it stay with her. She goes with Jesus to share her story, to share the Gospel. This is the tragedy many of us can fall in to: we are miraculously cured and freed, but instead of taking our redemption story to the people still sick and in bondage, we try to hide that we were ever in a position to need the miracle at all.

I began to wonder why it is we do this, and God gave me this picture: Jesus breaks every chain that's on you. It's broken, you're free, but you also have free will.
If you want to wear broken chains, you can.

The sad reality is that Satan tries to keep us trapped by convincing us that the broken chains can never really come off, that though they may not be who you are, they're who you were and that matters. But this is a LIE.

"This means that anyone who belongs to Christ has become a new person. The old life is gone; a new life has begun!"
2 Corinthians 5:17 NLT

The broken chains you're still wearing do not belong to you, woman of God. Step out from beneath their weight. We have lost sisters that need your story.

Reflection:

- Is there anything in your past that Satan is using to make you feel discounted?

- Are there any "broken chains" that you are still wearing?

- What has God set you free from? Have you ever shared that story? If not, why? Write a prayer asking God to give you the boldness to share the story of how He set you free. Ask God to point you to the women in your life that need your story.

DAY THIRTEEN

MARY MAGDALENE

PART ONE:
WOMEN WERE THERE

MARK 15

The curtain of the temple was torn in two from top to bottom. And when the centurion, who stood there in front of Jesus, saw how He died, he said, "Surely this man was the Son of God!" Some women were watching from a distance.

Mark 15:38-40a

NIV

After Luke 8, the next place we see Mary Magdalene is at the crucifixion of Jesus.
During my time studying Mary Magdalene, I noticed something I had never noticed before: the crucifixion story mentions women a lot. The main focus is of course on Jesus, but the two other groups talked about are the Roman officers & Jesus's female followers.

I began to wonder why the Bible didn't mention any of Jesus's male followers being there: Did none of them show up for fear of being killed? Was it just supposed to be understood that they were there?

Then it hit me ... maybe women were the only ones mentioned because God wanted to make sure that women knew He was talking to them.

In my Religion courses at UNA, my professors always told me that if you want to understand a Scripture, you can never look at that Scripture alone. You have to look at everything else around it to get its context.

In Mark 15, right before we're told about the women being there, we're told two things: 1. The curtain in the temple that separated humans from God was torn in two, and 2. Jesus truly was the son of God.

The placement's intentionality suddenly became clear. In the time of the New Testament, women were not allowed to converse with men who weren't their husbands, which probably made Jesus's female followers seem like harlots and rebels.

When the curtain was torn, it was saying that humanity no longer had to go through a priest to talk to God. They were now welcome into a real relationship with God; the fact that the scripture about the women comes right after that is like Jesus personally saying, "Women of God, you are not excluded from this. I ripped this curtain to get to you too, and if anyone has any doubts, you can tell them the son of God said so."

God truly does love His daughters. If I've learned anything studying the women of the Bible, it's that Jesus never treated women as less worthy, less useful, or less important than men. Jesus didn't ask women to be part of his 12 Disciples because that was His inner circle. He was protecting himself from temptation and any appearance of evil, and we should do the same with our inner circles. But, Jesus DID invite women to follow Him; Jesus DID invite women to do ministry with Him; and Jesus IS inviting you today.

For the longest time I thought that invitation was complicated and intimidating because I thought Jesus would be sending me to my "Jerusalem" by myself, but that's not it. Just like the women in Mark 15, Jesus isn't sending you out alone; He's inviting you to come with Him.

Reflection:

- Have you ever felt disqualified because you are a woman?

- Do you believe that God wants to use you?

- Where do you feel like Jesus is inviting you to go next? In other words, what is your next step? Write a prayer asking God to reveal to you what area He would like you to elevate your faith in. Ask Him what your next step is in your journey growing closer to Him.

DAY FOURTEEN

MARY MAGDALENE

PART TWO:

THE SAVIOR'S MESSANGER

MATTHEW 28

So the women hurried away from the tomb, afraid yet filled with joy, and ran to tell his disciples. Suddenly Jesus met them. "Greetings," He said. They came to Him, clasped His feet and worshiped Him. Then Jesus said to them, "Do not be afraid. Go and tell My brothers to go to Galilee; there they will see Me."

Matthew 28:8-10

NIV

The final place we see Mary Magdalene is in Matthew 28, and this is my personal favorite part of her story. Jesus had been crucified, and Mary Magdalene was going with Jesus's mother to prepare His body for burial. When they arrive, they do not find Jesus there. Instead, they find an angel from Heaven who gives the women the most important message that would ever be delivered. (28:7-8 NIV)

I think this is such an amazing moment in Scripture. Jesus has just risen from the dead; the Gospel has just been written, and the first people to ever share that message are two women of God! I absolutely love this: the first messengers to ever be sent out with the Gospel were women. Throughout Scripture, there are so many things intentionally put in by God to shut out our doubt. Women of God, you are undeniably called to share the Gospel.

The angel says something to the two women in this moment that I believe is a promise that we have when we are sent to share the Gospel: You will see Jesus show up when you deliver the message. (28:7 NIV)

Mary Magdalene certainly does see Jesus show up. On her way to tell the disciples the Good News, Jesus appears to her. She is the first person to see Jesus alive after the Crucifixion. You would've thought it would've been Peter or John, but no, it was her. He chose Mary Magdalene, the one who was once possessed by seven demons but was now sharing what Jesus had done for her, and what does Jesus do when He sees her? Reaffirms her calling. (28:9-10 NIV)

Maybe you feel like you don't bring much to the table. Maybe you have a past. Maybe you believe there are people more qualified that should be called instead of you.
But Jesus has shown up and given you a message to deliver. The message is the Gospel. The message is your testimony, your story. The message is what it meant when you met Him, what He did for you, what He saved you from, who He is and who that means you are. He's saying, "Don't be afraid! Go tell them so that they can see me."

The question is, will we go?

Get ready, Women of God, the Savior has a message for you to deliver.

Reflection:

- Have you ever felt disqualified to share the Gospel or share a Word that you heard from God?

- Do you regularly share the Gospel and/or your testimony? If not, why so?

- What's your testimony, Woman of God? Take the space below to write about it. Then, write a prayer asking God to give you the boldness to share it.

DAY FIFTEEN

JUDGES 4

PART ONE:
REALIZING WHAT YOU'RE IN

Sisera, who had 900 iron chariots, ruthlessly oppressed the Israelites for twenty years. Then the people of Israel cried out to the Lord for help.

Judges 4:3

NLT

Judges 4 is an amazing story of how God used two women mightily.

God's people were ruthlessly oppressed for 20 years before they cried out to God for help. When I first read that, I was quick to judge them, wondering why on earth they would wait so long before turning to God. Then I realized it could've been for 1 of 2 reasons: 1. They didn't realize what they were in, or 2. They didn't realize what God was doing.

Sometimes in the midst of a storm it can be easy to not realize what you're in the middle of, especially when, like the Israelites, we are caught up in living our own way. We stop seeing things through the spiritual perspective we have been gifted with and become short sighted. We forget that the oppression of God's people will always happen, and it is always spiritual (Ephesians 6:12 NIV).

Perhaps the Israelites spent 20 years fighting a spiritual battle with earthly means. Maybe they tried to use their own wisdom to get out of it, their own strength to fight it, their own resources to keep going, and came up empty, as we all do when we fight this way.

Once they had expended all of their energy, tried everything they could think of, it finally hit them: I can't win this battle on my own, but I know the One who can.

We are not the warrior; we are the weapon.
A sword cannot accomplish much on its own, but in the hands of a warrior, there is victory. This is why it makes sense that we need the Lord's strength, the Lord's wisdom, the Lord's power as we fight, because like the sword, we are the weapon wielded by the warrior to deliver the deadly blow to the enemy.

Woman of God, you are a weapon in the hand of the warrior who always wins.

Reflection:

- How do you respond when you enter a tough season?

- Do feel tired from carrying the weight and responsibility of trying to fix the situation rather than placing the situation in God's hands?

- Are you ready to release this from your control completely so that God can have it? Write a prayer asking God to help you trust Him with this situation. Ask Him to teach you how to be the weapon in the warrior's hand rather than striving to fight on your own.

DAY SIXTEEN

JUDGES 4

PART TWO:
REALIZING WHAT GOD IS DOING

Then Deborah said to Barak, "Get ready! This is the day the Lord will give you victory over Sisera, for the Lord is marching ahead of you." So, Barak led his 10,000 warriors down the slopes of Mount Tabor into battle.

Judges 4:14

NLT

There is a second reason it may have taken the Israelites 20 years to cry out to the Lord for help: They didn't realize what He was doing.

Perhaps the Israelites found themselves in a position I'm sure we all have at one point or another: in the midst of oppression, a storm, a hardship, and immediately asking to be removed from it.

Maybe the Israelites had been talking to God during those 20 years. Maybe they had been asking for Him to take the oppression away, to remove them from it. I've been there.

We don't like discomfort. We don't like inconvenience. So, when we're faced with it, our first response does tend to be "Stop it." But maybe God was actually doing something in this oppression, as He always is.

See, God is not a waster. If He is allowing pressure to be on you, it is to produce something that was not there before.
If you continue reading, the Lord sends word through the prophet and leader, Deborah, telling the Israelites they are about to be given victory over their oppressors *in battle*.

Here's what we should note: If the Israelites had not been oppressed, they would not have wanted to go to battle. Maybe our oppression is getting us ready for a fight.

I believe that when the Israelites finally cried out for help in verse 3, it was not to remove them from their oppression, but to be with them during it, to help them through it. Perhaps they caught glimpse of what God was doing.

If God had sent word that they would have victory over their oppressors before they made this turn, to ask God to be with them during this instead of removing them, they would not have relied on Him during the battle. They may have even allowed themselves to think that they created the victory themselves.

God is so intentional. Every detail is on purpose.
Let Him be with you, shape you in your hardship. Victory is not far away.

Reflection:

- Are you in the middle of a tough season right now? If not, think about a time when you were. How did you handle it?

- Ask yourself, what can I feel this hardship producing in me? Perhaps it's patience, faith, boldness, perspective, trust, leadership, etc.

- How has your attitude towards God been during the hardship? Have you been angry or hurt? Write a prayer asking God to give you a glimpse of what he is doing. Ask him to allow you to see what this hardship is producing in you and help you lean into it rather than run from it.

DAY SEVENTEEN

DEBORAH & JAEL

PART THREE:
FIGHTING FOR THE SAME KINGDOM

JUDGES 4

So, on that day Israel saw God defeat Jabin, the Canaanite king. And from that time on Israel became stronger and stronger against King Jabin until they finally destroyed him.

Judges 4:23-24

NLT

Deborah was a prophet who was judging Israel in Judges 4. The Hebrew word translated as "judge" actually translates better as "ruler / leader" or "deliverer from potential or actual defeat." [e]

There are so many things I love about Deborah's story. She was a leader, heard clearly from God, allowed God to use her, exhibited wisdom and authority, showed bravery, the list goes on.

She is someone I have admired in scripture for a long time because she shows that Women of God are called to lead. Yes, men are designed to be the leaders of our households, but women can still lead.
One definition of leader I found is "someone who can see how things can be improved and who rallies people to move toward that better vision." [f] I believe women are fully capable of this. They can get a vision from God of something better and rally people to that vision.
This is what Deborah did. This is what we all can do.

My favorite part of how Deborah led is something I did not see until I started this series. See, in verse 9, Deborah says that victory will come at the hands of a woman. If you don't read the entire chapter, it could be easy to think she is talking about herself, especially when it was her that Barak asked to come with him to battle. I believe she also could have made this woman herself. Since she knew how the victory would come, I believe she could have intervened and taken the victory for herself, but Deborah didn't do that.
No, instead Deborah allows Jael's story to be written. Jael killed Sisera, the ruler oppressing Israel, and brought victory to God's people.

e: Encyclopædia Britannica, inc. (n.d.). *Judges: Importance and role*. Encyclopædia Britannica. Retrieved November 16, 2021, from https://www.britannica.com/topic/biblical-literature/Judges-importance-and-role

f: John, A. S. (2020, January 13). *What is leadership, and who is a leader?* Chief Learning Officer - CLO Media. Retrieved November 16, 2021, from https://www.chieflearningofficer.com

I think this says a lot about how women should lead: championing one another.

As women, it can be easy to fall into comparison, which leads to competition. We feed our insecurities as we allow society to pit us against one another.

We so quickly forget that a victory for her, is a victory for me because we fight for the same Kingdom.

Satan would love for you to believe that her gifts, her success, her favor somehow lessens yours, but that is simply not how the Kingdom works.

No, in our Father's Kingdom, all His daughters are beautiful, all His daughters are chosen, all His daughters have purpose, and all His daughters will be used to advance the kingdom.

We all get good gifts in this house.

Here's the thought I'll leave you with: Perhaps Satan tries so hard to pit women against each other because women united would destroy him.

4:24 NLT "from that time on Israel became stronger and stronger against King Jabin until they finally destroyed him."

Reflection:

- In what ways can you practically lead the people around you?

- Do you struggle with comparison fueled competition?

- How can you champion the women in your life? Write a prayer asking God to show you how you can lead and champion the women around you. Ask him to silence the voice of comparison.

DAY EIGHTEEN

BLEEDING WOMAN, DAUGHTER OF THE KING

DELIBERATE PURSUIT

LUKE 8:40-56

But Jesus said, "Someone deliberately touched Me, for I felt healing power go out from Me."

Luke 8:46

NLT

I really fell in love with this woman's story. Every time I read it, it becomes more and more beautiful, intentional, and relatable.

She had struggled with her bleeding issue for 12 years. This number is important for two reasons: 1. It shows that it doesn't matter how long you've struggled, Jesus offers healing and freedom that is instant, and 2. The number 12 in scripture is used to represent the whole kingdom of God. It mirrors the 12 tribes of Israel (which Judaism was born from) and the 12 Disciples (which were sent to preach the Gospel to the gentiles), so in other words, it encompasses all Jews and all gentiles, the whole world. So, no matter who you are, no matter what you've struggled with or for how long, Jesus can heal it.

I saw something when I was reading that jumped out at me: Luke 8:46 NLT "But Jesus said, "Someone *deliberately* touched me, for I felt healing power go out from me.""
Deliberately.
The woman did not release the power of God from accidentally or unintentionally encountering Jesus. She did not release power by simply attending a church service unexpectant or by letting someone tell her about Jesus instead of her searching for Him herself.
No, the woman released the power of God by *deliberately* touching Jesus. She went after Him with everything inside of her and reached out for Him as if it was the only thing worth doing. I want to live like that.

Maybe you have something in your life that needs the power of God. Maybe you feel like you've been striving for so long that you don't have it in you to reach out very far. Well, here's another beautiful part of her story: she only had the strength to reach the hem of His robe.

God does not have unrealistic expectations for us. Jesus came to earth and lived among us so that He could sympathize with you about how hard it really is. But if you can just touch the hem of His robe ... See, God's power is not reliant on our strength or ability; it just requires a deliberate reach towards the King.

Here's what you can expect once the power is released. The woman received healing instantly. She already received what she was hoping for, but Jesus wouldn't let her go unnoticed. He sought her out because she came searching for a physical healing, but Jesus had something else to give her: identity.

No one understood why He would search through a sea of people for someone who touched Him, but He would go to any length to look into her eyes and say, "Daughter" (Luke 8:48 NLT).

For 12 years she had been "bleeding woman," but now, she was daughter of the King. I'm not sure what you may believe about who you are, but woman of God, you are a daughter of the King. Imagine the power from Heaven we could release when we become deliberate in our pursuit of Him, embracing who we truly are.

Reflection:

- What area(s) of your life need the power of God?

- Which Identity do you live in: Daughter of The King or "Bleeding Woman"?

- Are you deliberately pursuing Jesus daily? Write a prayer asking God to help you be intentional in your pursuit of Him. Ask Him to help you live in your true identity and access His power.

DAY NINETEEN

MARY OF BETHANY

THE ONE AT JESUS'S FEET

LUKE 10:38-42

Her sister, Mary, sat at the Lord's feet, listening to what He taught.

Luke 10:39

NLT

Luke 10:38-42 NLT

38 As Jesus and the disciples continued on their way to Jerusalem, they came to a certain village where a woman named Martha welcomed him into her home. **39** Her sister, Mary, sat at the Lord's feet, listening to what he taught. **40** But Martha was distracted by the big dinner she was preparing. She came to Jesus and said, "Lord, doesn't it seem unfair to you that my sister just sits here while I do all the work? Tell her to come and help me."

41 But the Lord said to her, "My dear Martha, you are worried and upset over all these details! **42** There is only one thing worth being concerned about. Mary has discovered it, and it will not be taken away from her."

It's disheartening how many things in this world are trying to pull us away from the feet of Jesus.

It's all grasping for our attention: politics, news, social media, relationships, comparison, the list goes on and on. Some of the things fighting for our attention aren't even bad things. Helping her sister prepare a meal for Jesus would not have been a bad thing, but it wasn't where Mary's focus needed to be.

What has your focus been on lately?

I've found it very easy recently to turn my attention and energy to the wrong things, and it has left me exhausted. Maybe you've felt exhausted too.

The beautiful thing, though, is that there's a place we can bring our exhaustion that will never be taken away from us: the Feet of Jesus.

No matter what happens around us, no matter what is fighting for our attention, the feet of Jesus are always available to us. Learning from Him, being with Him, is the only thing worth being concerned about. If we do that, everything else will fall into place.

No matter how hard we try, we cannot control anything. But we can position ourselves at the feet of the One who already controls everything.

Matthew 11:28 NIV "Then Jesus said, "Come to me, all of you who are weary and carry heavy burdens, and I will give you rest.'"

The King is inviting you back to His feet, where you can make a trade that could never be earned: Your Heaviness for His Rest.

Reflection:

- Are there things, concerns, habits, or people in your life pulling you away from the feet of Jesus?

- Are you exhausted?

- When was the last time you truly laid *everything* at His feet? Write a prayer surrendering everything that has been consuming your focus and energy. Tell Jesus you trust Him with it more than you trust yourself, and ask Him to give you true rest.

DAY TWENTY

ABIGAIL

INTERCEDE

1 SAMUEL 25

David replied to Abigail, "Praise the Lord, the God of Israel, who has sent you to meet me today! Thank God for your good sense!

1 Samuel 25:32-33a

NLT

Abigail has a story that I had never read until I started this study. She did something that takes a lot of courage and humility. She decided to intercede for someone who, honestly, didn't deserve it.

Abigail was the wife of Nabal. Nabal was foolish, ill tempered, mean, and crude (the Bible's words not mine). King David had always been good to him and his servants, so when it was sheep shearing time, King David asked Nabal to share some of his many provisions with him and his men. Nabal said no, in a very rude way, and this infuriated David. He gathered his men and set out to kill Nabal and all his men.

Some of Nabal's servants heard this and ran to tell Abigail. There were probably a lot of thoughts that rushed into her head. A part of her may have even wished this on Nabal because he had been so terrible over the years, but she didn't even entertain those thoughts.
1 Samuel 25:18 NLT says, "Abigail wasted no time." She knew what she was called to do. She knew that vengeance was the Lord's, and her job was simply to intercede, even though he didn't deserve it.

I wonder how many more people I would've interceded for if I didn't entertain any of the "but they" thoughts. God always has the same response to those anyway. But they hurt me, God. Intercede. But they don't deserve it. Intercede. But they would NEVER do this for me. Intercede.

Something God has taught me through interceding for someone who hurt me is that it is way more about changing your heart than it is changing them.
When you pray blessings on the people who've hurt you most, Jesus begins to show you what He did for you.
Jesus died for me even though time and time again I would hurt Him and choose sin. I certainly didn't deserve someone interceding for me saying "forgive her because she doesn't know what she's doing," and yet, Jesus did that because He loved me.
Jesus will show you how to love them the way He loves them by showing you the way He loves you.
"Forgive as the Lord forgave you" Colossians 3:13 NIV.

Abigail ran out and met King David and talked him out of murder. This was not an easy thing to do. She could have easily been slaughtered, but David recognized that the Lord had sent her. When we intercede for those that have hurt us in prayer, it becomes obvious who sent us.

There's certainly nothing easy about praying blessings on those who've hurt you, but it makes it all the more powerful. When we stand in the gap for someone else, Heaven sees it and rewards it.

The vengeance truly was the Lord's because Nabal has a stroke and dies when he hears what Abigail did and how David responded. Here comes the really beautiful part, though. David decides to marry Abigail.
She was hoping to be his servant and got to become his family.

It's truly beautiful to me to see God go above and beyond, like He always has.

David would've saved her by making her a servant, but he decided to give her more.
Jesus would've simply saved us by dying on the cross, but He decides to offer us more.

We get to be daughters, we get to be vessels, we get to be messengers, we get to be intercessors, we get to be more because Jesus says to us "My love is more than enough" (2 Corinthians 12:9 AMP).

Woman of God, Jesus says you're called to be more, so intercede.

Reflection:

- Who is God calling you to intercede for?

- What stops you from interceding for them?

- Have you forgiven those who have hurt you? Write a prayer asking God to help you forgive, knowing that forgiveness does not excuse what happened. Ask Him to give you the faith to pray blessings upon them.
  Spend some time interceding for those who God lays on your heart.

DAY TWENTY ONE

SHATTERED PRIDE

GETTING THE FATHER'S ATTENTION

Going through the motions doesn't please you,
a flawless performance is nothing to you.
I learned God-worship
when **my pride was shattered**.
Heart-shattered lives ready for love
don't for a moment escape God's notice.
Psalm 51:16-17 (MSG)

You do not desire a sacrifice, or I would offer one.
You do not want a burnt offering.
The sacrifice you desire is a *broken spirit*.
You will not reject a broken and repentant heart, O God.
Psalm 51:16-17 (NLT)

I've never thought of being broken as a good thing. According to the Cambridge English Dictionary [g], being broken means to have "suffered emotional pain that is so strong that it changes the way you live."

Perhaps they're on to something. Perhaps the emotional pain that we are supposed to feel in order to change the way we live is the gut-wrenching shattering of our pride.

Pride is finding fulfillment in one's own achievements. I can see why that is so dangerous. If we for a moment think that it is us accomplishing anything, we have missed the point.

True, I can do everything ... through Christ (Philippians 4:13 NLT). If you leave off the second half of that Biblical statement, you're only left with a disappointing delusion. When you add the second half, you'll have purposeful power.

Sometimes I think the obvious direction to go with pride is towards the "I accomplished this. I did this. I deserve the praise," and yes, that is very dangerous.
More often than not, though, I find myself on the other side: unfulfilled pride.

There is another danger to thinking you are the one accomplishing, and it comes when the thing does not get accomplished. When we find our fulfillment in our own achievements, how are we left feeling when we do not achieve?

g: "Broken." *BROKEN | Definition in the Cambridge English Dictionary*, dictionary.cambridge.org/us/dictionary/english/broken.

How can I be a more effective tool in the hand of God? Live with my pride shattered.

I must remind myself every day that my fulfillment is not in the outcome of what I may be involved in here on earth, but in what the Savior decided I was worth.

I do not accomplish, God does. Therefore, if I am feeling inadequate or unfulfilled, it is not an indication of my failure, it is an indication that my pride has grown back.

"Heart Shattered Lives ready for Love Don't for a moment Escape God's Notice" Psalm 51:17 MSG

I want your notice, God; teach me to re-shatter my pride.

Reflection:

- In what areas do you struggle with pride?

- How can you practically shatter your pride daily?

- Do you find worth in your achievements? Write a prayer asking God to help you put on humility in all things. Ask Him to remind you that your worth is not dependent upon what you can achieve.

DAY TWENTY TWO

THE FATHER

MATTHEW 26

He went on a little farther and bowed with His face to the ground, praying, "My Father! If it is possible, let this cup of suffering be taken away from Me. Yet I want Your will to be done, not Mine."

Matthew 26:39

NLT

At one of Church of the Highlands' First Wednesday services during Communion, I thought of something I've never thought of before.

Communion has always been a place where I focused on Jesus, God the Son. And it should be, "Do this in remembrance of me" (Luke 22:19 NLT) are pretty clear instructions.

This time during Communion, though, I found myself thinking about God the Father.

Specifically, I found myself in the Garden, in the last conversation between father and son before Jesus would be killed.

Matthew 26:39 NLT "He went on a little farther and bowed with His face to the ground, praying, "My Father! *If it is possible, let this cup of suffering be taken away from Me. Yet I want Your will to be done, not Mine.*"'

I thought about these words as I have many times before. How hard it must've been for Jesus to say them, but ... *how hard it must've been for The Father to hear them.*

I don't have children yet, but I serve children on Sundays, and I thought about how it breaks my heart when I have to do something that upsets them. I know it will be so much more heartbreaking when I have to tell my own children "No."

Then I thought, what if it was my only child, the only child I would ever have, and what if their question that I had to say "No" to is "Is there a way I don't have to die?"

How the Father must've felt as he told his only son "No."
Then I remembered something just as bewildering: the "No" was for me.

The "No" the Father spoke in this conversation was so that we could be made right with Him, so that we could become His children, so that we could share Jesus's inheritance.

The Father sacrificed His perfect child to save His broken ones.

Reflection:

- Take some time and reflect on the sacrifice that was made for you. Thank God the Father for sacrificing Jesus for you. Thank Him for His vast love. Thank Jesus for His obedience. Let the Spirit of Adoption rest on you. Express your gratitude for the nature of our God's heart.

DAY TWENTY THREE

MARY
MOTHER OF JESUS

CALLED TO BE BRAVE

LUKE 1

Mary responded, "I am the Lord's servant. May everything you have said about me come true."

Luke 1:38

NLT

Thinking about Mary: She was really brave, like *really brave*.

I mean she was only around thirteen years old and got told she was going to become pregnant and give birth to the Savior. I'm a married twenty two year old and that would've freaked me out. Not to mention she could've been killed, dragged into the streets and stoned to death kind of killed.

She could've been disgraced, not to mention the disgrace she would bring on her family. She could've lost everything. Her reputation would be shattered because no one would be assuming she got pregnant by the Holy Spirit.

These were all things Mary knew. But her response was simply, "I am the Lord's servant." (Luke 1:38 NLT)

See, Mary had a Heavenly perspective on her situation. Instead of seeing the opposition, she saw the opportunity.

She didn't let the idea of what people might do to her distort the vision she had of what God might do through her.

Her focus was on the right "What if?"

I wonder what I might do, what we all might do, if we combated every earthly "What if" with a Heavenly one.

"What if I offend them?" -> "What if it saves them?"

"What if they don't listen?" -> "What if this starts their story?"

"What if they judge me?" -> "What if they need me?"

"What if I don't know what to say?" -> "What if God uses me as His messenger?"

"What if they've heard this all before?" -> "What if this time the harvest is ready?"

"What if this ruins our relationship?" -> "What if this is their last chance?"

Today I pray for a new boldness in all of us, that the heavenly "What if" would begin to silence the earthly one. God give us a sense of urgency, give us a heart for Your lost kids.

Women of God, you are called to be brave.

Reflection:

- Is God calling you to anything right now that will require you to be brave?

- What stops you from sharing the Gospel/ your Testimony with someone?

- Pray and ask God to give you a fresh boldness.
  Use the space below to write out the "What if" thoughts that hold you back and then combat them with a Heavenly "What if."

DAY TWENTY FOUR

ELIZABETH

FILLED WITH THE HOLY SPIRIT

LUKE 1

At the sound of Mary's greeting, Elizabeth's child leaped within her, and Elizabeth was filled with the Holy Spirit. Elizabeth gave a glad cry and exclaimed to Mary, "God has blessed you above all women, and your child is blessed."

Luke 1:41-42

NLT

There are so many things that I could talk about with Elizabeth's story, but the one that jumped out at me the most was that she was filled with the Holy Spirit.

Sometimes I think it is easy for us to take the Holy Spirit for granted. We kind of forget that He's there, or we forget that He is God. We forget that He is the one giving us power and authority, the one who is our comforter, teacher, and reminder of who we are.
Perhaps this is just me, but I know that I don't access Him enough.

The thing I love about Elizabeth is that she accessed the Holy Spirit and allowed Him to use her. Through the Holy Spirit, she was able to encourage Mary, prophecy over her, bless her, and see beyond the physical.

Mark 13:11 NLT "don't worry in advance about what to say. Just say what God tells you at that time, for it is not you who will be speaking, but the Holy Spirit."

How much more beneficial would the things I say be if I offered Him my voice every single day, not just when I'm speaking, teaching, or writing on the Word of God, but for every moment of my life.

Women of God, we are called to access the Holy Spirit: to become His mouthpiece, to utilize His power, to walk with His authority, and to see beyond the physical.

Reflection:

- What does your relationship with the Holy Spirit look like?

- If you don't know much about the Holy Spirit, spend some time reading about Him in God's word. Here are some verses to get you started: John 14:16-18, 25-27; Mark 13:10-11; Luke 11:9-13; Luke 10:21; Luke 24:44-49; John 20:21-22; Acts 1:4-8; & Acts 2 NLT.

- Pray and ask the Holy Spirit to reveal Himself to you. Ask for a fresh anointing of the Holy Spirit, and ask God to help you access His wisdom, peace, boldness, and power.

DAY TWENTY FIVE

THE SAMARITAN WOMAN

LEARNING WHO JESUS IS

JOHN 4

Jesus replied, "If you only knew the gift God has for you and who you are speaking to, you would ask Me, and I would give you living water."

John 4:10

NLT

The Samaritan woman has such a beautiful story. It's one that I see myself in a lot.

7 Soon a Samaritan woman came to draw water, and Jesus said to her, "Please give me a drink." **8** He was alone at the time because His disciples had gone into the village to buy some food. **9** The woman was surprised, for Jews refuse to have anything to do with Samaritans. She said to Jesus, "You are a Jew, and I am a Samaritan woman. Why are you asking me for a drink?"
10 Jesus replied, "If you only knew the gift God has for you and who you are speaking to, you would ask Me, and I would give you living water." John 4:7-10 NLT

I began to think about this interaction, and I realized I've had this exact conversation with Jesus before myself. "Why do you want me, God? You shouldn't want anything to do with me. I'm not worthy."
The beautiful thing is that Jesus says to me exactly what He said to her: "If you only knew the gift God has for you and who you are speaking to"

See, Jesus wasn't concerned with the reasons the woman had to disqualify herself from His presence. He didn't want her to continue living in sin, as He addresses later in the chapter, but He was not there to shame her. He was there because He had something to offer.

I think so often we disqualify ourselves from God because we think we're the ones that are supposed to have something to offer, but Jesus is saying, "No, I'm the one with the gift for you, and when you truly grasp hold of the reality of this gift, you'll know who I truly am."

This gift is not transactional, conditional, or dependent on you in any way. You can't earn it, and therefore, you can't disqualify yourself from it either. Jesus is not a salesman; He is love.

It has become clear to me that every time I show up to Jesus with all my reasons that I am not worthy, I break His heart. Because if I truly think that He would ever see me as unworthy, I don't know who He is.

The King of Kings has a gift for you, one you can neither earn nor disqualify yourself from: to replace your cares with a crown, your loneliness with love, your past with His presence, your heaviness with hope, and live the way He always wanted you to: with Him.

Reflection:

- Do you find yourself feeling unworthy?

- Do you ever hold yourself back from God's presence because you feel unworthy of it?

- Do you know that every thought of disqualification is a lie? Write a prayer asking Jesus to help you see yourself the way He sees you. Ask Him to replace those feelings of unworthiness with His love.

DAY TWENTY SIX

MARTHA

DELAYED, NOT UNANSWERED

JOHN 11

But when Jesus heard about it, He said, "Lazarus's sickness will not end in death. No, it happened for the glory of God so that the Son of God will receive glory from this." So, although Jesus loved Martha, Mary, and Lazarus, He stayed where He was for the next two days.

John 11:4-6

NLT

Martha is another woman in the Bible that I feel like got an unfortunate reputation because of one instance where she just wanted to prepare an amazing meal for Jesus and wanted her sister to help her with the work. I mean I know she missed the point of that moment with Jesus in that story, but come on. That's relatable. If my sister was my roommate and Jesus was coming to our house and she wasn't helping me cook, I'd be bitter too.

Martha is honestly one of the most relatable characters to me in the Bible when I look at her closely. I find this to be especially true in John 11, when her brother dies.

Martha had asked Jesus to show up. She knew that if He came, her brother wouldn't die, but Jesus didn't come when she wanted Him to. Maybe this is something you can relate to.

Jesus waits to go to Lazarus, and he dies. Martha is devastated and confused, but she still wants to hold onto her faith. When Jesus arrives, she runs out to meet him and says, "Lord, if only you had been here, my brother would not have died. But even now I know that God will give you whatever you ask." (11:21-22 NLT)

I don't know about you, but I've found myself in this moment many times: wondering why God let this happen, wanting to question, trying to keep a grip on my faith, trying to trust. This was Martha.

She knew that Jesus could perform miracles, but the reality she was standing in was that her brother was dead, and it looked like Jesus had come too late.

She still trusted Jesus, though, because after she leaves the conversation with Him she goes to get her sister and brings her to Jesus. I love this about Martha: in the midst of her confusion in what the King was doing she still brought people to His feet.

After talking with Mary, Jesus weeps, showing how much He truly cares, and then goes to the tomb of Lazarus. He tells them to remove the stone, and this is when something very interesting happens: Martha protests.

Have you ever felt angry that your prayer didn't get answered the way you wanted?
It can be easy in the midst of grief and loss to lose sight of who exactly Jesus is. Martha was concerned about the smell since Lazarus had been dead for days. Perhaps you have a dream, something you once prayed for, buried in tomb that has been there so long you're afraid that if Jesus dug it up, it wouldn't be any good anymore. But let me remind you, we serve a God who is still in the business of calling dead things back to life.

My absolute favorite part of Martha's story is something she never even gets to know. As soon as Jesus hears of Lazarus's sickness, He says to His disciples, "'Lazarus's sickness will not end in death. No, it happened for the glory of God so that the Son of God will receive glory from this." So, although Jesus loved Martha, Mary, and Lazarus, He stayed where he was for the next two days" (11:4-6 NLT).

Perhaps your request has not been denied. It has been delayed for the glory of God, and although Jesus loves you so much, He needs you to wait a few more days.
He wants to give you more than a yes; He wants to give you a miracle.

Reflection:

- Are you feeling frustrated with the way a prayer was answered, or perhaps, with the lack of an answer?

- Do you have a dream, promise, or prayer "buried in a tomb" that you have lost faith in? Perhaps it's time to let Jesus dig it back up.

- What is a higher priority to you, the prayer being answered the way you wanted or God being glorified? Write a prayer asking God to help you trust Him and believe that whatever the answer may be, it is in your best interest and for His glory. Ask God to revive your faith as He resurrects those buried dreams, promises, and prayers.

DAY TWENTY SEVEN

REBEKAH

AN ANSWERED PRAYER

GENESIS 24

"O Lord, God of my master, Abraham," he prayed. "Please give me success today, and show unfailing love to my master, Abraham. This is my request. I will ask one of them, 'Please give me a drink from your jug.' If she says, 'Yes, have a drink, and I will water your camels, too!'—let her be the one you have selected as Isaac's wife.

Genesis 24:12 & 14

NLT

I felt prompted to write about Rebekah, but at first glance, I didn't know where God was going with her story. It seemed like she was just the beautiful girl that would marry Isaac, a secondary character, but then something caught my attention: she was an answered prayer.

Abraham sent his servant to go get a wife for Isaac, and the servant prayed that the woman he was supposed to return with would do more than what he asked her. He would ask her to give him some water, and she would do that plus water the camels. If Rebekah had not gone above and beyond or if she had been in a hurry, she would not have been the answer to his prayer that God intended for her to be.

I began to think about my own life; I wonder how many times I've missed what God was doing because I wanted to do the bare minimum, or I didn't slow down long enough to realize that God might want to do more.

The Shoals Campus Pastor of Church of the Highlands, Caleb Chambers, gave our church's interns a list of things to challenge us with at the beginning of the Fall 2021 semester, and the one that I've been trying to work on is: Walk Slowly through the Crowd.

I've quickly come to realize that there is always a task at hand, but God is always wanting to do more.

People are always God's priority, so they should be mine as well. Jesus was never in a hurry to get anywhere, and I believe that was because He knew the people in between where He was and where He was going mattered. They were placed on the path from here to there on purpose because that's where they would encounter Jesus.

There are people purposefully placed on your path from where you are to where you're going so that you can be the vessel through which they encounter Jesus.

But you can't deliver a message you don't know that you have, you can't have a message unless God gives you one, God doesn't give you one unless you're listening, and listening only happens intentionally.

Someone is asking God for something, and you just may be who He's sending to answer them.

If Rebekah had been in a hurry, focused on her tasks, wanting to do the bare minimum, she simply would not have been the answer to the servant's prayer.

I want to be the answer to someone's prayer.

Reflection:

- Do you often find yourself in a hurry or aiming to do the bare minimum?

- What are some practical things you can do to help you slow down?

- Do you make room/time for God to use you in your day-to-day life? Write a prayer asking God to help you slow down and steward the people He has placed on your path. Ask Him to use you to be the method through which someone encounters Him.

DAY TWENTY EIGHT

STAY WITH THE CLOUD

EXODUS 40:34-38

Now whenever the cloud lifted from the Tabernacle, the people of Israel would set out on their journey, following it. But if the cloud did not rise, they remained where they were until it lifted.

Exodus 40:36-37

NLT

Transparently, there have been many times in my life where I have battled the fear of "missing it." Missing God's timing, missing God's purpose, plan, intention, lesson, opportunity, just missing it. As I read Exodus 40:34-38, I was reminded of a beautiful, weightlifting truth: My responsibility is not to make sure I don't "miss it." My calling is to stay with the cloud.

So often I think we get overwhelmed with the worry that we need to catch up to God, as if God is at the final destination, and you are on a train. We stress over making sure we don't miss our stop, but the reality is that our Heavenly Father has been the conductor the whole time.

You will not miss your stop. Sometimes God is calling you to remain where you are until HE is ready to move. Don't rush past His intentional pause. I would much rather arrive at my destination with the King of Kings than by myself.

I love that the book of Exodus ends this way: a picture of the Lord guiding His people. The Word says that at night, the cloud would have a fire glowing inside of it so that the whole family of God could see it, and God did this for ALL of their journeys. No matter the season, whether a dark or a light one, God will guide you through. He will not leave you. The cloud never outran the Israelites, it never left without them. When God begins to move, He will let you know.

Until then, ask Him why you're stopped. What would you like me to do here, God? What would you like to cultivate in me, teach me, show me while I'm here, God?

Lord, give me an expectation to see you move in my life even when the cloud is not lifted.

"The Lord directs the steps of the godly. He delights in every detail of their lives. Though they stumble, they will never fall, for the Lord holds them by the hand. Once I was young, and now I am old. Yet I have never seen the godly abandoned or their children begging for bread." Psalm 37:23-25 (NLT)

Reflection:

- Do you battle the fear of "missing it" in your life?

- Have you fully surrendered your timing and received God's timing in exchange?

- Spend some time in prayer being honest with God about how you've felt. Repent for not trusting His timing and receive His overwhelming grace. Ask Him to give you fresh vision and renewed peace.

DAY TWENTY NINE

ENTER IN

ISAIAH 6

Then one of the seraphim flew to me with a burning coal he had taken from the altar with a pair of tongs. He touched my lips with it and said, "See, this coal has touched your lips. Now your guilt is removed, and your sins are forgiven."

Isaiah 6:6-7

NLT

One day during one of our worship services, I was feeling unworthy. I found myself dwelling on all of the mistakes I had made just that morning. Perhaps you've been here before. I was standing there, wanting to engage in worship, but wouldn't let myself into the Throne Room of God's presence because I felt disqualified.

The Holy Spirit whispered to me, "Unclean lips will not withhold My presence from you. It's in My Throne Room that you receive the cleansing."
I felt his grace wash over me as He brought Isaiah 6 to my mind.

It is within His presence that our desperation for Him is recognized. It is within His presence that we realize the parts of us that need to be cleansed, and it is within His presence that we receive the fresh coals of cleansing.

I love that the angel did not stop Isaiah at the door in Isaiah 6. He didn't tell Isaiah to clean his lips before he entered into God's presence. It was God's presence that revealed to Isaiah just how desperately he needed the cleansing.

The Lord will not withhold His presence from you on account of your mistakes. In fact, He ripped the veil trying to get to us while we were still shouting "Crucify Him!"

I believe the Lord is stoking hot coals just for you every single day, waiting for you to enter into His presence to be cleansed, forgiven, restored, and then given fresh purpose.

My favorite part of Isaiah 6 has always been Isaiah's response to the cleaning: Here I am. Send me. The Lord response to Isaiah, I believe, is His response to you and me: Yes, Go, and Say to this people.

If you want God to use you, He will. If you want God to send you, He will. If you want God to give you the words to speak, He will.

But to receive any of this, we cannot withhold ourselves from His presence.

Enter in, Daughter. He has been waiting for you.

Reflection:

- Do you find yourself feeling disqualified from God's presence?

- Do you know in your heart that the Lord is not mad at you when you sin, He just misses you?

- Spend time pursuing God's presence. Ask Him for fresh cleansing, forgiveness, restoration, and purpose. Pray for the intimate friendship of the Holy Spirit to become tangible in your life.

DAY THIRTY

HULDAH

A MESSAGE TAKEN SOMEWHERE

2 CHRONICLES 34:26-28

So, they took her message back to the king.

2 Chronicles 34:28b

NLT

"But go to the king of Judah who sent you to seek the Lord and tell him: 'This is what the Lord, the God of Israel, says concerning the message you have just heard:
You were sorry and humbled yourself before God when you heard His words against this city and its people. You humbled yourself and tore your clothing in despair and wept before me in repentance. *And I have indeed heard you, says the Lord.* So, I will not send the promised disaster until after you have died and been buried in peace. You yourself will not see the disaster I am going to bring on this city and its people.'"
So, they took her message back to the king.

2 CHRONICLES 34:26-28 NLT

Huldah's story shows up in two places in the Bible: 2 Kings 22 and 2 Chronicles 34.
In both places, King Josiah sends his men to consult with Huldah, the prophet, concerning the scrolls of scripture they found. She tells them what God had said, and in both books, it says, "So they took her message back to the king."

I couldn't stop thinking about those words "So they took her message back to the king." I wasn't sure why at first, but then I thought about how Huldah heard God so clearly. In the Bible, it doesn't say that the king's servants got there, asked her about the scroll, and then she had to go pray and ask God what he thought. No, it says they showed up and she spoke. Meaning that she had either already heard from God His opinion on the matter, or the Heavenly Father was speaking through her as she spoke. After she spoke God's message, it was taken somewhere.

I think I got hung up on that line because I thought about the messages God would speak through me, the messages God would speak through you, and where they would be taken. Will they be taken back to a king? A President? A hurting person? A broken heart? A lost soul? A wayward child? A woman just discovering her calling?

Here is what I know: the Lord has a message for you to deliver. He wants to speak so clearly to you, through you, that it will seem impossible. Then, the message will be taken somewhere because in Isaiah 55:11 NLT the Lord says, "It is the same with My word. I send it out, and it always produces fruit. It will accomplish all I want it to, and it will prosper everywhere I send it."

We may not know where the message will be taken to, but isn't it amazing to get to be the messenger?

Reflection:

- What are your expectations for your devotional time with God? Do you hear from Him every day? He desperately wants you to hear His voice daily. He is not holding back.

- What message/testimony has God given you to deliver? Are you expectant that God will do something miraculous with the message?

- Write a prayer asking God to speak to you clearer than He ever has before. Ask Him to give you a message to deliver and then give you the faith and expectancy to believe that He will do something miraculous through it. Ask Him to increase your boldness.

Made in the USA
Coppell, TX
18 September 2023